Thylacoleo Lives

Dennis Wright

This book originally published in Australia by
D.A. & M.E. Wright
Email: damewright@hotmail.com

Conditions of sale

Thylacoleo Lives

Introduction

I first produced "Thylacoleo Lives" as a booklet in 2002, because of numerous sightings reported to me and questions asked by witnesses. I became interested in the topic after seeing a strange panther like animal at Tarnagulla. I had previously seen one many years ago from a great distance but it was when I experienced the animal in close proximity I realised this was something unique.

The booklet has grown to be a book because of numerous additional sightings, including several of my own, and a state government enquiry that has been conducted since the first publication. The number of additional sightings and other information since gathered has provided a much greater understanding of these animals and further supports my hypothesis that we are dealing with a remnant of the genus Thylacoleo Carnifex.

Thylacoleo Lives

Chapter 1

Light grey shades had begun to appear in the Eastern sky but in the West the stars still shone brightly. It was the midst of a hot spell and even before dawn the temperature was comfortably warm. The day was predicted to be close to forty Celsius so I crawled out of my sleeping bag and out of the tent.

I had brought a couple of friends to do some prospecting in the old diggings of the Victorian gold fields. The area I had taken them was near the township of Tarnagulla where numerous nuggets of one to two ounces had previously been found within inches of the surface. We set up camp by the river a couple of kilometres from where we had been using metal detectors to locate any pieces of gold missed by the old miners. My friends were city raised and not used to getting up before dawn so I decided to leave them asleep and take my rifle to see if there was anything worth shooting. If I could not find any game worth bagging I would be content to eliminate a few feral pests.

I poured a coffee from the vacuum flask I had made up the night before and took some cheese and a hardboiled egg from the car fridge and by the time I had finished these it was light enough to be able to see any animal I might want to shoot. I climbed through the fence beyond the campsite and began to follow the river. The light was improving rapidly, no long drawn out twilight periods in Australia, when the sun rises or sets it does so rapidly.

I rounded a bend in the river and a flock of large grey ducks were foraging in the paddock I raised my rifle and looked through the scope, but decided I did not feel like plucking ducks so I put it down again. A tortoise saw my movement and jumped off his log into the river, causing a slight splash and sending ripples up and down the stream. I continued my trek along the riverbank, just below the rim so that only my head and shoulders were visible above the bank.

There came the sound of dogs barking and agitated from a farm house almost two kilometres across the paddock, and I knew they were not barking at me because I was too far away. The house had the usual collection of machinery sheds, stockyards and shearing shed but from among some trees and bushes near the shedding I saw an animal. It was obvious that this was what had upset the dogs and I immediately thought, "Wow I am going to bag a panther," the 'Bealiba beast' as it had become known due to numerous sightings near that town.

The animal even at my distance was clearly visible, it was large and judging its height by the fence it was running beside it had to be at least ninety centimetres tall at the shoulder, this was no feral cat. It was the height of a full grown sheep and longer. I slipped the magazine from my rifle and fully loaded it with fifteen rounds and left the one in the chamber making a total of sixteen rounds that my semi-automatic rifle could fire in less than seven seconds. Having this rapid fire ability I could stop even a charging animal fairly quickly, I had used it on foxes and seen the animal rear up at the first shot while I hit it at least twice more before it hit the ground.

I had absolutely no fear of facing a panther just the shock of being hit rapidly by a dozen bullets, even though I was only using lead bullets and not full metal jackets, would stop a bull or a wild boar even if it did not kill them instantly.

Taking stock of the area I realised the animal was following the fence line and that the fence and the river converged about a kilometre or more ahead. I decided that I would remain obscured below the level of the paddock and move in on the animal where the river and fence came together. There were game trails along the bank so the going was clear and quiet and sometimes my head was visible above the bank but no more of me was visible.

The animal's gait could only be described as bounding, it seemed to use its hind legs together and leap forward landing on forelegs one first and then the other before bunching its body as the hind legs landed then again leaping forward. The movement was fluid and seemed to be a relaxed pace that could cover many miles with little effort.

At one point the animal stopped and looked back in my direction, even though it could not have seen me, heard me or smelled me because we were moving into the wind and it was forward of my position. I was reminded of the old trick of staring at the back of a person's head and have them turn around; the animal appeared to have sensed me looking at it even though I could not be seen. I have hunted many animals and this is an unusual trait.

I had been stalking the animal for about thirty to forty minutes moving along the river. The animal drew ahead as the fence line was straight and the river curved in places meaning that I had further to walk. It reached the junction of the fence and river and easily jumped the fence taking up a position under a large river gum and sat preening itself while watching for whatever it was sensing to get close.

By the time I eventually I ran out of cover and had to move in to the open to continue my approach. The animal was catching the first rays of the rising sun; it saw me but ignored me continuing to lick its black shiny coat, it showed no fear. I reached a point about twenty-five metres from where the animal sat and I thought, "keep preening you idiot you are about to become a trophy and put to bed the rumours of panthers in the Australian bush".

I slid the safety off and slowly raised the rifle, avoiding sudden movements that might spook the animal. Looking through the scope with the crosshairs right between its eyes I got the shock of my life. This animal was **not** a cat, it was totally and obviously a marsupial; first cousin to a kangaroo, a one hundred and fifty kilogram meat eating possum. I stood there stunned and decided against being the person who might make such a rare and amazing animal extinct.

My first thought was, "This animal is a native; it belongs here." I lowered my rifle and watched the animal for another minute or two and then I decided to see how close it would let me get so that I might better examine the unusual sight. It appeared to be ignoring me as I approached by about another ten metres but then my path was blocked by a washout and a large tree.

In order to move closer I would be forced to either go down into the washout and up the other side or pass behind the tree. I chose going behind the tree as the easiest and quickest option and in the two seconds it took me to step around the tree the creature vanished. I looked at the spot where it had been now only about fifteen metres away and thought, "How could it get away from there without me seeing it?"

There was little cover and a lot of open space it would have to traverse to get away and I could see no sign of the animal, or anything that would provide cover for so large an animal. I spent quite a while circling round and looking for a den or some sort of cover and could find no way that the animal might have escaped. I eventually gave up and headed back to camp, cursing the fact that I had not had a camera.

It was some years later that I received the information that explained how the animal could so magically disappear. A tour bus was travelling through the Grampians region of Victoria when the driver and several passengers saw a panther cross the road in front of the bus. The driver stopped as quickly as possible just past the point where the animal had crossed the road and people ran back with their cameras but it was nowhere to be seen.

After searching for several minutes one of the passengers spotted it; leaping through the treetops like an overgrown possum or a tree kangaroo. On hearing this report I realised then how the animal I had seen had so easily disappeared. I had conducted a fairly extensive search but had not looked up into the treetops.

My sketch of Thylacoleonid creature seen near Tarnagulla, the fence is shown in the background to provide an idea of the approximate size.

Chapter 2

The first evidence of Thylacoleo Carnifex (Marsupial Lion) consisted of fossilised bones found in caves in Wellington N.S.W. The bones, which included strange teeth, were sent to England where Professor Richard Owen who examined them, identified and named the species in 1859. The most recent example of Thylacoleo remains discovered has been determined to be at least seven thousand years old. It has therefore been concluded that Thylacoleo must have become extinct at that time.

Scientists are unable to provide a satisfactory answer as to why such a large and successful predator should cease to exist. Despite two hundred years of settlement reports are still received which indicate that we have yet to identify Australia's entire unique fauna. Since the earliest settlement reports of large "cat like" predators abound. Some reports state that these creatures have been heard to "roar like a lion" as do koalas, and despite the large number of sightings science refuses to accept the existence of such an animal.

This refusal by science is based on two precepts;
1. No specimen has been shot or captured.

2. No recent remains have been discovered.

My research has produced explanations, which can account for both of these paradigms.

1. Reports of sightings occur mainly at dawn, dusk or night, which indicates that the animals seen are nocturnal hunters. Australia's population is almost twenty four million of which over 70% live in major or capital cities. The remaining 30% live in small towns or rural areas at an average density of 1.26 people per km^2. The true population density in rural areas is much lower as people tend to live in towns leaving millions of km^2 with zero population, in rural areas few people travel around the bush after dark.

A nocturnal species has vast uninhabited tracts of land to wander undetected; it is surprising that it is ever sighted.

2. The Aboriginal inhabitants of Australia conducted what is known as "fire stick farming" in that they regularly fired forests to promote new growth and encourage breeding of their prey animals. The regular burning would have destroyed any animal remains, which were not protected. Thylacoleo is arboreal and we believe may live in large hollow trees. A body in one of these would be completely incinerated in a bushfire. The interior of a hollow tree can burn with the intensity of a blast furnace.

Reported sightings of these large predators are received from all over Australia, in Queensland most sightings are of a large striped animal commonly called the Queensland Tiger Cat.

In the Blue Mountains of N.S.W. and most of Victoria, the predominant sightings are of a black, panther like animal. The black "panther" is commonly reported in many other states, and appears to be the most frequently seen animal.

Positive identification of animals sighted is further complicated by the large number of introduced species. In addition to bringing horses, camels, sheep, cattle, cats, dogs, rabbits and foxes early immigrants may have brought other more exotic creatures. Asian Gold Cats (*felis temminki*) have been reported and may have been brought with other Chinese traditions to the early goldfields. Feral cats have grown to very large sizes and have done more damage to indigenous wildlife than almost any other import except possibly the rabbit which has not only destroyed unique flora, but caused the starvation of countless small marsupials.

University of Ballarat historian Dr David Waldron is in two minds about the existence of big cats. On one hand, the lack of proof in the form of carcasses claimed as road kill, after bushfires, or through illness and death, belied their presence, he said. "But, given the sheer numbers that have been brought to Victoria and subsequently released into the wild, I can't believe they haven't overrun the state like foxes or rabbits," Dr Waldron said. Dr Waldron appears to have been the first academic to have uncovered legitimate big cat sightings and hunts dating back to the 1870s.

From as early as the 1860s to the 1940s when Australia imposed strict quarantine laws, classified newspaper advertisements boasted of tigers, lions, monkeys and other exotic animals for sale in cages on the docks at Footscray. A large number of sightings of the American Mountain Lion or Puma occur in Western Victoria in a large area centred on the Grampians Mountains. There is no official record of how these animals came to be in the area but researchers have established from eyewitnesses the source of this population.

A contingent of U.S. Marines was based at Victoria Park in Ballarat during WW11; they had with them their unit's mascot a female Puma. During their stay, the puma gave birth to four (?) cubs and when the orders came to ship out to Guadalcanal in 1942, they were ordered to destroy the puma and her offspring.

The soldiers disobeyed and took the puma family to a farm near Moyston Victoria and released them into the bush, returning every three days with food. On their third visit only a week before leaving, the puma family had already left the area. The farmer on whose property the animals were released has since died and no further living witnesses are known, it is possible that some American Servicemen who were present may still be alive, but as it is now over seventy-five years since the soldiers shipped out the numbers will be dwindling.

In addition to this report Bulletin Magazine reported in January 2004 that the Deakin University study had located three eyewitnesses' with accounts of American airmen with pumas in 1942. Two were in the Mount Gambier region of South Australia and one was at Nhill, two Australian guards at Nhill had remembered a USAF bomber landing with a puma cub on board. The cub was allegedly taken to the Grampians and set free.

The Deakin University study was headed by Dr John Henry a lecturer at the science faculty, his final report filed away in the university library provides some intriguing details. Among the facts discovered were the following interesting discoveries.

1. In the rugged Geranium Springs Valley sheep carcasses were found on a ledge three hundred metres above the valley floor.
2. Mutilated carcasses were also found on the valley floor.
3. Droppings recovered were identified by a leading US expert as consistent with puma scats.

4. Within a rock shelter many animal remains from large cattle bones to tortoises were found.
5. Researchers took casts of two large carnivore footprints which US experts judged as matching those of a puma.

Dr. Henry has maintained the study's conclusion that it is beyond a reasonable doubt that a population of big cats resides in the Grampians.

These sightings tend to confuse reports of other animals and add to the general scepticism that surrounds all reports creating an atmosphere, which discourages witnesses from coming forward. In Victoria, there are five reported sightings every day and when inquiries are made researchers discover that only about ten percent of sightings are reported. Almost every person who reports a strange animal knows of several other people who have also seen it but never reported it. Extending this data, we conclude that in Victoria about 18,000 people see these animals each year.

In addition to the striped "tiger cat", black "panther" and pumas we have reports of thylacines (Tasmanian Tigers) being seen in various parts of the country. Australians are very familiar with the appearance of the thylacine.

The Cascade Brewery has this creature as its logo and images are common. It is possible but very unlikely that the striped cat like animal could be mistaken for a thylacine. The thylacine is very dog like and unlikely to be compared to a cat. In Queensland, the striped "cat" has been seen to climb trees a skill unknown in thylacine. It is also noted that when climbing down a tree this animal comes down tail first, like a koala, and not head first like a cat or possum.

**Cascade Brewery Logo features
Thylacine.**

**Queensland Tiger Cat is distinctly
different from Thylacine.**

The summation of all this is that there appears to be several order of cryptid creature in Australia. The first is the puma apparently left behind by American servicemen or imported before 1940. The second is the thylacine; whether an indigenous variety or an introduced species transported from Tasmania is unknown.

Tasmanian Devils were found living in the bush in Victoria and again we are unable to ascertain whether they were indigenous or imported. The third appears to be a genus of thylacoleo, which apparently, has at least two sub-species.

It is the thylacoleo, which is the subject of this book, and why I and others believe the mysterious black "panther" is a species of thylacoleo; what we know of its lifestyle and what it looks like. Most of the sightings and research in this book relate to Victoria but the conclusions are just as relevant to sightings in other states.

Chapter 3

This book is written with so much certainty about an animal which science claims no longer exists because as well as my experience detailed in chapter one I have seen the animal on other occasions. My first sighting was when I was still in primary school, my brother and I had arisen early one morning and gone for a walk in the bush.

It was just after dawn and we were walking along the ridge line when we saw the animal cross over the ridge and move down into the timber in a gully. It was only visible for about a minute but that is a long time when one sees a large panther like predator. Although it was well over a kilometre away from us we turned around and went home, we were both young and unarmed.

Growing up in the Victorian bush, I had heard stories of the "panthers" since I was a young boy. Neighbours had seen them and family members had known of them since the days of the gold rush. In those days, I was just as sceptical as everyone else but that first sighting wiped that away however my real interest did not develop until my very close encounter and the realisation that this animal was not a cat; no matter how like a panther it appears.

Probably the first time I had heard about the animal was when a neighbour had a guest from the city staying for a holiday. The guest wanted to go shooting so our neighbour loaned him a gun and directed him the direction to take. It was a simple route following a gully upstream for a couple of kilometres and then turning around and following it back down again to arrive home.

The guest was only gone a short time when he came back as pale as if he had seen a ghost and shaking with fear. The neighbour took him in and sat him down with a cup of tea while he asked what had upset him so much. The neighbour came over later and talked to my father about it and his comment

was, "He saw the Bunyip." "What's a
Bunyip?" I asked, and was told that this one
is big like a lion but black. I knew then that
the guest had seen the same animal
witnessed by my brother and me.

A subsequent sighting happened in company
of other witnesses so I can be very sure that
none of us was mistaken. I was going
shooting with my brother Trevor and his
friend Geoff. We were accompanied by my
son James and two of his friends Allan C
and Allan W and the father of Allan W,
Allan W Snr. I knew Senior fairly well and
had been sailing with him as well as
shooting and prospecting trips, unfortunately
he is now deceased but my other
companions are still alive and can attest to
the accuracy of this report.

We had travelled to my parent's property
and borrowed a utility to carry us into the
bush. The seven of us planned to go to a
major gully together then each take a
separate branch into the hills in which to
hunt. Deer, goats and pigs are not unknown

but not common in this area but it abounds with other feral animals mostly rabbits and foxes.

We parked the utility near the head of the main gully and set out as a group, we had plenty of time because it was still fairly dark. The sky was beginning to go grey with the promise of dawn but visibility was still somewhat limited and so we travelled slowly through the bush in the dim light. The first branch gullies were several hundred metres up the main gully, past an old dam built during the gold mining days, but now part silted up to be very shallow.

We passed the dam and continued for a short way when Allan W Junior said, "What's that?" He was pointing at a dark object just visible in the early dawn light; his father looked and then replied, "It's just a kangaroo." It did look like a kangaroo sitting on its haunches with a long thick tail and it was the right size, about shoulder height to a man. "I saw it walking and it is not a kangaroo." Responded Allan Junior, so I suggested, "Fire a round behind it so we can see what it is."

He raised his rifle and aimed at the ground just above the animal's tail. The bullet struck sending a handful of dirt and gravel flying all over the animal which jumped up and bounded away; as soon as I saw it move I recognised the gait as being exactly the same as the animal that I had seen near Tarnagulla years before. It leaped off taking only a dozen long bounds before reaching a patch of scrub and timber and becoming lost from view.

We completed our hunting trip without catching another glimpse of this elusive animal.

Chapter 4

I have been fortunate enough to catch glimpses of these animals on several other occasions. In the late 1980's there had been several reports of sheep predation in the Tyaak area; at the time my wife and I operated a café at Broadford so elected to go out after closing in the hope of seeing the predator.

It was a week night and so we closed about nine PM and cleaned up so that shortly before ten we were ready to take the four wheel drive and go to the area the stock losses had been occurring. My wife myself and a daughter took the things we thought we might need and headed out in the hope of seeing whatever had been eating the stock. We let ourselves in the farm gate we had arranged and found the flock of sheep camped under some trees near the top of a hill.

We travelled on past the sheep and stopped on a hill opposite and where we had a reasonable view of the gully and opposite hillside in the dim light of a just rising last quarter moon. The night was clear and cool and we opened the windows enough to hear the night sounds while we watched for any movement. We had been sitting watching for about forty minutes when I heard a commotion coming from where the sheep were encamped.

Putting up the windows and starting the car I drove down through the gully and up to a point just below where the sheep had been bedded down. The sheep were no longer there; instead they were below us on the hill and milling around in the corner of the paddock obviously spooked by something we could not see. I hopped out of the car for a better look around and my wife and daughter did the same.

I was holding a camera but the flock was too far out of range for the flash so I walked a little way toward them hoping to be close enough to take a picture if I saw what was frightening the sheep. I had moved about ten metres from the car when an animal jumped the fence and grabbed a sheep. The flock scattered in all directions and I knew that I would need my spotlight if I was to get a picture.

I raced back to the car yelling, "Quick I need my spotlight!" The women had already been as frightened as the sheep, jumped in the car AND LOCKED THE DOORS. I was standing there locked out without my spotlight and a camera that was useless while the animal picked up a fully grown sheep and dragged it back over the fence and carried down into the scrub along the gully. One of my best chances to have obtained photographic evidence went begging.

Several other brief sightings have resulted in me just missing out on the definitive photograph. One was near Tallarook at dusk, I was driving on a quiet back road and the animal was near the side of the road it started bounding off and by the time I stopped and grabbed the camera it had vanished in the gloom.

On one occasion near Maryborough it was late afternoon and had been raining, the sun broke through and I decided to go for a walk. I took my grandson's little Australian terrier and my video camera and headed into the forest. The dog was running ahead with his nose to the ground excited because following rain dogs love to hunt, every scent is a fresh scent.

The dog was about fifteen metres ahead when all of a sudden it froze, then turned around and with its tail between its legs bolted for home. I wondered to myself what had so spooked the dog and moved forward. There on the top of a mullock heap watching something below was a 'panther' I snapped the cap off the video camera and it heard me move; as I turned on the power the animal jumped away to my right. I raced to the top of the mullock heap hoping to be able to film it but it was out of sight. I watched and then saw birds rise in panic as some bushes about eighty metres away moved and I realised the animal was moving about four times as fast as I could.

Admittedly I had been running uphill but in the time I covered twenty metres it had gone eighty. I looked down to see what had been attracting the animal's attention and saw a prospector with his metal detector and headphones, totally oblivious to the panther, the dog or me.

It occurred to me at one time that maybe a means of travelling through the forest quickly and quietly might just be the way to get close to one of these animals and get good quality photographs or video. I got my mountain bike out of the garage and taking my video camera I started taking early morning rides. I did surprise many unwary kangaroos and wallabies and on one occasion got close to our elusive predator.

It had been raining but because there had been sightings I was not going to let that stop me. I rode several kilometres through the bush without luck and so turned for home I had been riding about a kilometre on my return trip when the now familiar black shape and bounding gait crossed the track in front of me. I raced to the spot and jumped off my bike.

I couldn't see the animal but I could smell the wet animal smell of his passing. Taking out and turning on my video I started to follow the scent, noticing a couple of large animal footprints in the fresh mud that showed I was on the right track. I followed the scent and tracks for about a hundred and twenty metres they led to a copse of large iron bark trees.

I had long suspected that these may well be suited to thylacoleo because their black bark would provide perfect camouflage for a black arboreal animal. Just as koalas favour trees with bark that is the same colour as their fur, or alternatively evolve to have fur the right colour to provide camouflage so too it follows that a black thylacoleo would favour the iron bark trees with their dark colour.

I searched through the tree tops but was unable to spot the animal either on the ground or in the trees and so had to eventually give up my search. I consider myself lucky to have seen these animals six times but considering that I have spent most of my seventy plus years in the bush this represents a sighting about once every ten years. To those people who think the existence of these animals is impossible my advice is to find a job where you spend a lot of time in the bush; particularly late at night or very early in the morning, and within ten years you will probably see one. My sightings have always been either just before dawn or after sunset, I have never seen one during the day. One sighting close to town happened very late at night but as it is my most recent sighting I will include it with some other local sightings toward the end of this book.

Chapter 5

Thylacoleo is believed to be arboreal, that is, it climbs trees. This fits in well with reports of the striped Queensland animal, which has been seen climbing. In a previous chapter I mentioned a report from the Grampians, area of Victoria where a 'panther' was seen high in the treetops; it was leaping from one tree to the next. This is extraordinary behaviour for such a large animal and demonstrates a high level of awareness, to be able to judge the strength of branches. Australian sub-tropical forests are often not as densely woven as are those in the wetter tropics and suitable branches are often well spaced.

People often say that it would be impossible for such a large creature to remain hidden. I then tell them the true story of a circus elephant lost at Maryborough in the 1990's. The circus was camped on the edge of town and during the night the elephant pulled free of its chains and headed off into the forest looking for food. Despite a thorough search

43

next morning the elephant could not be found. The circus had to pack up and leave town without their elephant but local residents were urged to be on the lookout for an elephant wandering in the forest.

The elephant was found over three months later when a local householder woke to find an elephant eating their garden. The circus was notified and sent an animal trainer and truck to collect the wayward beast. The moral of the story of course is that if a tame elephant can remain hidden for three months how much easier for an elusive nocturnal predator to remain hidden. It is a wonder that these animals are ever seen.

I also compare thylacoleo to possums which although much smaller are similar in nature, anatomy and habitat. We can walk through the bush all day and never see a possum, but go out after dark with a good light and they are surprisingly common; thylacoleo may also be reasonably common.

Chapter 6

Once I began to make inquiries I initially found only people who had seen the animal but finally a farmer had an altercation when he cornered a "panther" but it charged him and escaped. The episode made news headlines the poor farmer was ridiculed but a research group came to his support. I contacted the President of the organisation and told him that it was not a cat and described what I had seen.

He directed me to have a look at some publications about various Australian animals past and present, on completing the research he suggested I was able to ring him back and tell him that I had seen a thylacoleo. He said that he had believed that was what I observed but did not want to influence me into claiming something that I had not seen. He also relayed to me the story of a young lad who surprised a black animal in the bush. The animal growled at him and showed its teeth, the picture the lad drew of

the teeth he had seen matched the dentition
of thylacoleo.

After seeing the animal when in company of
a large group I realised that the animals are
not quite as rare as I had first thought, and
so I began an active search for them. I have
spoken to many witnesses examined kills
and seen tracks. Every piece of information
adds to the record and brings us closer to
finding proof positive that Thylacoleo is not
extinct.

The thylacoleo is considered extinct, its
demise believed in some circles to have
occurred with the mega fauna about forty
thousand years ago. Some other evidence
has suggested that it might have much
longer and have been gone for at least seven
thousand years, because no remains have
been found that are more recent. It is
probable that thylacoleo lived until more
recently as there is some evidence which
points to this fact. Dr. Gill (former Curator
at Melbourne Museum) wrote in a paper
many years ago that there were bones

bearing marks similar to those attributed to thylacoleo dentition that had been made "horizons after thylacoleo". This paper was part of a discussion on the feeding habits of thylacoleo and whether marks on a bone fragment could have been made by a thylacoleo. The concept that these marks were made after thylacoleo was considered extinct must be reviewed if thylacoleo is alive and well, as many thousand eyewitnesses believe.

Aboriginal legends of the "drop bear" speak of a current animal and not something from the distant past. The drop bear is reputed to drop from a tree onto its prey below. This hunting technique has only ever been attributed to one Australian animal, thylacoleo. The legends say that the drop bear has been known to kill people.

There is no conclusive proof that thylacoleo has not attacked humans as many people have disappeared in the Australian bush and never been found. Their bones may be lying undiscovered or may have been devoured. A body in an area where Tasmanian Devils exist will not last long; these friendly little chaps devour everything. Devils will kill but usually just eat carrion they devour skin, bones, hair and even clothes. The picture on the next page, found at Drysdale River, Kimberley, WA, appears to show a hunter defending himself from a thylacoleo. Is the folktale of the drop-bear 40,000 years old or has thylacoleo survived until today?

In a study published recently in the Nature Journal, Scientific Reports researchers reveal they have found thousands of claw marks etched on the interior of a limestone cave. This cave, named Tight Entrance Cave, is situated near Witchcliffe, WA. What they found adds new substance to the gradually emerging picture of thylacoleo carnifex's physique and behaviour.

The researchers recorded and analysed the size, shape, depth and angles of the scratches. From this the palaeontologists were able to deduce previously uncertain aspects of the marsupial lion's biology, the large number of smaller scratches in the cave hints at how thylacoleo raised its young.

Picture: D. MacLeod / Akerman & Willing

Examining scratch marks in the cave researchers conclude, "The largest of the scratch marks could only have been made by adults of thylacoleo carnifex", researchers say. "Many of the smaller marks were made by juveniles: they have the same form as that of the adults, but do not match claw marks made by other known cave dwellers." It is believed that caves would have offered the cool and safe environment needed. Underground lairs also could be defended from other carnivores such as thylacines (Tasmanian tigers) and Tasmanian devils.

The drop bear method of attack on a prey is another clue in the effort to prove thylacoleo exists. Recent predation of kangaroos has been discovered where the carcass is beneath a tree with a horizontal branch and the kangaroo has been killed by a blow, which has broken the neck and caved in the back of the skull. A one hundred and fifty kilogram animal leaping onto one from many metres above is almost certain to inflict these sorts of injuries.

Thylacoleo only hunts at night and encounters with people are rare. In areas of central Victoria where sightings are most common, the following is a summary of instructions given to people who are concerned about coming face to face with a thylacoleo.

A sighting at sunrise means he has probably already eaten and is safer to approach, very cautiously. Unless he is interested in you he will just disappear, if he disappears, look up. Do not walk under his tree; do not act aggressively. The only person reported to have had a bad experience with Thylacolco was the farmer who cornered and tried to shoot one. Thylacoleo escaped by charging the startled farmer. Other close encounters have seen people run away when Thylacoleo snarled at them, he has never chased anyone.

Reports from the 1800s claim aggression from large cat like predators, these reports mainly originate in Queensland. Should you happen to walk through the forest where he is hunting he will growl; we recommend you leave. Thylacoleo does not hunt humans, but aboriginal legend says the drop bear has killed people. If you are ever unfortunate, enough to become the prey of Thylacoleo you will be dead before you even know that he is there. He will probably drop from a tree using his weight to break your neck.

This is a most effective ploy as skeletons discovered suggest that thylacoleo could weigh up to 260kg ($^{1}/_{4}$ ton). In addition to sabre like teeth, the Thylacoleo has a hand like a possum with an opposable thumb. The thumb is equipped with a folding dewclaw, up to four centimetres long and which springs out like a flick knife.

Chapter 7

Our knowledge of the anatomy of thylacoleo is derived primarily from fossil remains and secondly from eyewitness descriptions. No zoologist or veterinarian has ever examined a living specimen, so a part of what we can derive is little more than speculation. It is also the reason that official government policy is that no such animal exists. The main identification noted by palaeontologists and eyewitnesses is thylacoleo's dentition, his teeth.

Thylacoleo has large "tusk like" front teeth and his molars are more like bolt cutters than teeth. In 1969 Mr. L. G. Rentsch a 75-year-old farmer from Byaduk in western Victoria gave the following description of a strange animal which he encountered while repairing a fence. He had seen the animal approaching from over two hundred metres away and hid among some bushes so that it would not see him and run away. It approached to within about ten metres before going through the fence and leaving the area.

Mr. Rentsch describes the creature as; "Very big, between three and four feet high and very long in the barrel. It had a head like a cat's - only bigger of course. It was grey and brown underneath. It had a white nose, which turned up in front of the eyes. It had round brown eyes and short round ears. It had two tusks protruding from its mouth but I don't know if they were from the upper or lower jaw."

Mr. Rentsch also noted that the tusks were about three inches back from the nose. This is consistent with many other observations and a renowned photograph of a thylacoleonid animal.

Miss Rilla Martin took one of the best
known photographs of an unusual animal in
1964. In Miss Martins photograph, shown
on the previous page it is obvious that the
nose extends further than the lower jaw.
This is a peculiarity noted by many
witnesses but not discernable from the fossil
record. Miss Martins photograph shows a
striped animal similar to the Queensland
striped marsupial cat. There are many
reports of striped animals not only in
Queensland but also in many other states.

The area where this photograph was taken,
Goroke near Horsham in western Victoria

has long been the site of many reports. The most frequently seen animal in the area is a striped creature commonly called the Ozenkadnook Tiger, named for a small town where it was first seen.

Chapter 8

In addition to unusual teeth, thylacoleo has distinctive paws. Ian L. Idriess the famous author and prospector described the forefeet of the Queensland cat, which he had seen. "Its pads were armed with lance-like claws of great tearing strength." Scientist Mrs. Eileen Finch described a thylacoleo skeleton found at Moree in N.S.W. "The paws were strong, heavily clawed and probably used in striking prey or for tearing it." In addition to the claws, thylacoleo has an opposable thumb, as described in a previous chapter.

Thylacoleo is a formidable predator whose size equates to that of a lion or tiger. He has sabre like teeth and lance-like claws it is fortunate that apparently even old thylacoleos are capable of hunting their regular prey and none has to our knowledge ever become a man-eater. Although Aboriginal legends and stories describe animals such as the "drop bear" which drop from trees and kill even unwary humans.

Sketch of thylacoleo produced by paleo-artist Jeff Johnson based on witness descriptions and fossil evidence.

Scientific study of fossil remains depict a creature that has a heavy head, very large somewhat cat like, wide with well-spaced forward looking eyes. A thick muscular neck supports the heavy head and the body and tail noticeably long. Its legs are long for its body size and the clawed hind feet are over 15 centimetres long (similar to the brush tail possum to which the thylacoleo is distantly related). The nature of the hind feet also indicates that thylacoleo is capable of climbing trees.

Photograph of 18cm footprint found in forest near Maryborough in Victoria.

The forefeet are completely different to the hind feet again similar to those of the possum they are capable of grasping and indicate the animal's ability to climb trees. The forefeet are comparatively long, narrow, and armed with sharp claws. The digits two, three, four and five cannot be widely separated but the first finger, or thumb is opposable. The thumb is larger than the other digits and is equipped with a large dewclaw three to four centimetres long.

Thylacoleo is not related to any cat but its skull has a superficial likeness to that of the African lion. The marsupial Lion is unmatched by any carnivorous mammal, either living or extinct. The unique dentition is what makes Thylacoleo one of a kind; his third premolar shows a specialisation unlike any other predator.

This tooth extends up to 57mm along the upper jaw and the outside of the counterpart in the lower jaw slides against the upper set's inner side in a shearing action. In addition to this action the teeth are higher in the front than in the rear, anything that thylacoleo bites is trapped as the mouth closes locking flesh or bone in a bite as effective as bolt cutters.

Chapter 9

The habitat of thylacoleo for many years was mainly open forest, which has a low number of very large trees per acre. Since white settlement most of the original forest has been cleared and the regrowth forests contain many more but smaller trees. The native animals appear to have adapted to this change in one area a possum species was found to have adapted to living in burrows. This acceptance of changed conditions also applies to the thylacoleonid species.

In mountainous country, where many old large trees remain thylacoleo has not made as much adjustment. In less hilly country, particularly in old goldfields areas there has been a lot of clearing but forests have returned as the mines closed. The new forests are much denser than the original but this may change as stronger trees begin to dominate and the weaker succumb to recurring drought.

It has been calculated that it takes about one hundred years for a new growth forest to restore to the original old growth density. The Department of Sustainable Environment decided to thin out some Victorian forests to make them more like the original open forest; the problem has been that for every tree cut down about four more have grown, these forests are now denser than ever. Thylacoleo has probably become more of a ground dweller in these areas, but if the forests are left with no further clearing in another hundred years they will return to their original density.

The arrival of white settlers has provided Thylacoleo with extra sources of easy to catch food, such as sheep and rabbits. Thylacoleo numbers may be increasing but their habitat is shrinking, pushing them into closer and closer contact with humans. If Thylacoleo were not nocturnal, we would have hundreds more people seeing them every day.

Changes in habitat may lead us to locate and photograph a thylacoleo during daylight hours. It appears that he does not live in a permanent den or location but is nomadic. Most sightings that occur at dawn occur near water, indicating that thylacoleo prefers to spend his days not needing to travel far to reach water.

A number of reported daytime sightings where "panthers" have been disturbed demonstrate the animal's adaptability. One was disturbed in an old car body and another was in a shed. In the bush another was disturbed under a pile of flood stacked logs. In each instance, the animal quietly moved on without fear or aggression. It appears that the species is not afraid of humans but does not want to associate with them. A number of reports indicate that the animals demonstrate some curiosity and will stop and watch people from a distance.

Because the animals are nomadic and hunt at night, they are very difficult to locate. All recorded sightings have been accidental; the animals have only been seen by people who have been working or walking in the bush and rarely by a researcher or hunter who has been looking for them. Tracks, predation and other evidence have been found confirming that the creature is around but a photograph or body has yet to be obtained.

Chapter 6

The most common way in which we
discover that Thylacoleo is in an area is not
by sightings but by predation. This means
that we find the remains of animals that he
has eaten. Thylacoleo's unique dentition has
already been detailed and this is how we
recognise animals that have been devoured
by thylacoleo. Cats, dogs and similar
animals have pointed teeth and chew bones
leaving indentations, thylacoleo's teeth
operate like shears occasionally leaving
slice-like marks on bones.

In areas where large cat like predators are
seen they are often blamed for many stock
kills for which they are not guilty. When
examining livestock kills researchers can be
sure that if more than one animal was killed
in a single night the culprit is almost
certainly a dog pack. Dogs prefer to hunt in
packs but even if a single dog attacks, he
will chase sheep or cattle until they are
exhausted and bite many more animals than
he kills. A dog or dogs will kill for fun once

they begin to chase and get the taste for blood.

Big cats are basically lazy; they hunt when hungry kill one animal and eat as much as possible. Big cats will probably then not eat for several days. If they kill a large prey animal such as a full-grown sheep or a cow they may return and eat more of the same animal later but are unlikely to hunt. Mature large cats such as the puma and panther can weigh from 33 - 100 Kg and are therefore not likely to eat an entire sheep, which may weigh 100 kg or more.

Thylacoleo may weigh more than twice as much as a puma and apparently has no trouble consuming a whole sheep in just one night; it may also be that they are cooperative hunters. In one example a farmer checked his flock one afternoon to ensure that all were well and that the paddock contained adequate feed and water. The following morning when he returned to move them to an adjoining paddock he was surprised to find one of his sheep had been killed and completely eaten. The body had been stripped clean; the meat had been removed from the bones as neatly as with a boning knife.

Only one known predator has ever had teeth capable of slicing meat from a bone in such a manner and that is thylacoleo. Australia has only ever had one predator large enough to eat a whole full-grown sheep. I examined the remains of this kill and could detect no evidence of secondary predation by foxes or other scavengers. There was also no sign of chewing on the bones as would be expected if the sheep had been eaten by a cat or dog. The only conclusion that could be reached was that this animal had become prey to a thylacoleonid creature.

I have been shown other animals and photographs of animals killed and eaten in a similar manner. Some I was shown quite recently are about forty kilometres from where similar kills happened almost twenty years ago. We don't know the life expectancy of these animals but the time and distance separation indicates that it is not the same animal and implies a breeding population.

Example of a sheep eaten overnight by a predator which appears to have thylacoleonid dentition

A similar recent report comes from the East Gippsland area of Victoria where a number of cattle were killed over a period of some months. The farmer had seen large black "panthers" in the area including one eating a heifer that it had killed. He described the carcass as not having been chewed or torn but having been "cut as if with a carving knife". This is an accurate description of the manner in which a thylacoleo would eat the flesh from its prey.

Researchers are normally only notified that a predator is in an area, when livestock are taken. Farm animals are not normally the prey of choice of thylacoleo. His main and apparently preferred prey is still the kangaroo and research indicates that many more kangaroos are taken than are sheep, goats or cattle. In areas, where thylacoleo has been detected by researchers who have discovered tracks, or been called by witnesses, the number of kangaroo kills can outnumber farm animals killed by ten to one.

It appears that thylacoleo also eats animals other than kangaroos and livestock. Some smaller creatures seem to have been taken but these are difficult to establish because they can be eaten whole. A rabbit or possum makes only a mouthful or small snack for an animal as large as thylacoleo.

In an area, where many tracks have been found and numerous animals killed I once found a large bird, (probably a grey currawong) which had apparently been eaten by a thylacoleo. When a bird is taken and eaten by a fox or a cat there is a tendency for feathers to be spread around the region where the bird was eaten. The bird, which I found, was completely eaten and no feathers were to be seen, the only remains were the wings. The wings were attached to each other by a small piece of sinew but appeared to have been neatly snipped off the body as though by a pair of shears.

I have on occasion found birds that have been killed by foxes and feral cats but in each case a large area was strewn with feathers. Once I was called to investigate the sighting of a puma and found tracks and other evidence including a hen which the puma was alleged to have taken. The puma had eaten the hen and even this large cat had left a telltale trail of feathers.

Chapter 7

In order prove the existence of thylacoleo researchers are working to create a proper database of sightings, stock kills, tracks and anything else that might help build a picture of regular movements. In the hope of calculating where one might turn up next and then have a camera ready to take his photo. Once a thylacoleo is confirmed in a region the government would be urged to create a sanctuary surrounding the area identified as its habitat.

Despite my efforts and records of reliable sightings and evidence and a data base compiled by NSW researchers who have a record of over two hundred and seventy recent sightings governments in both NSW and Victoria refuse to acknowledge that such an animal exists. The Victorian government did conduct a study in 2012 to assess the "Evidence for the presence of big cats". The study of concluded that there was no "primary evidence" *i.e.* a body or "secondary evidence" *i.e.* a clear photograph.

I compiled a submission of eyewitness accounts and photographs of predation and of animals that had survived attacks. The response that I received explained that "the study was in its final stages and the opportunity to include additional contributions had passed". In other words the result had been decided prior to the study being conducted. My input was ignored as "too late" even though it was sent in during the time allocated for public submissions.

For some reason governments are avoiding proper research into the question. In addition to ignoring my research they have ignored the research completed by Bulletin Magazine in 2004 and the work and the research completed by Deakin University in the 1970's. The government enquiry came up with a result that directly refutes all other research and countless eyewitnesses as well as the evidence of famers who continue to lose livestock to these supposedly non-existent creatures.

Experienced researchers are always careful to ensure that witnesses are not led to conclusions. It is often necessary to insist that what has been seen is a feral cat or a wombat or other common animal, if the witnesses falter and are not sure, the sighting cannot be regarded as genuine. People who clearly see a creature, which is unusual, will not be shaken from their story; they become very definite about what they have seen.

Witnesses who work in the bush and work with animals make very reliable witnesses and are unlikely to misjudge the size or nature of an animal. Witnesses who have reported seeing large predators and are considered extremely reliable include; police, farmers, forestry workers, Government employees from Departments of Agriculture, Mines, Tourism and National Parks and Wildlife, a Zookeeper and a veterinary employee. It is unlikely that people with the experience and responsibility of these positions would rashly make false claims or are prone to mistake any ordinary animal for a large panther like predator.

Chapter 8

Reliable witnesses and physical evidence appear to support the theory that thylacoleo is alive, well and living in the Australian bush. We have a reasonably accurate description of what it looks like and much of its behaviour. Some witnesses have also been able to provide additional insights into how the animal behaves.

One prospector who lives on the edge of the Wombat State Forest in central Victoria claims that a "panther" stays in the forest behind his home every spring, moving on in summer. He has seen the animal many times but only during spring. This type of information helps to build our knowledge and has enabled the following summary to be compiled.

1   Thylacoleo is usually black but striped animals are also regularly seen.
2   Thylacoleo is arboreal (tree climbing) and apparently prefers Ironbark or Stringy Bark trees.

3 Thylacoleo sizes can range from about 80kg to 260kg.

4 Almost all sightings are of a single animal, they are not overly gregarious and young apparently leave the mother fairly soon after leaving the pouch.

5 Thylacoleo is nomadic making tracking and locating difficult.

6 Thylacoleo hunts primarily at night but is sometimes seen travelling through the bush during daylight hours.

7 Thylacoleo is primarily a forest dweller but has adapted to stalking and capturing prey in open farmland.

8 Introduced species have become popular prey, but land clearing has provided more grazing enabling kangaroos to become more plentiful.

9 Thylacoleo numbers appear to be increasing but their habitat is shrinking.

10 Thylacoleo appears to be no threat to humans.

11 A single Thylacoleo may range across a territory of $400km^2$ (20km X 20km) which would mean that Victoria with an area of 227,619 km^2 of which about 60%

or 136,571 km^2 is suitable habitat and would possibly support a population of about 550 of these animals. Should they be able to live in smaller areas or in overlapping territories the population could be far higher.

Despite the obvious difficulty in tracking and proving the existence of an animal which has eluded capture for more than two hundred years researchers are still optimistic that a specimen will be photographed. Photographic evidence is seen as the first step in proving that thylacoleo has survived until the present. Properly equipped research can then commence to locate and tag an animal with an electronic transmitter to enable a complete study to be undertaken.

Sightings become more common during periods of drought when animals move out of the forests or rough country to find water. During the drought of the early 1980's and again in first half of the 1990's sightings were at a peak. With most of Australia, in the grip of drought in the early 2,000's many more sightings occurred before rain arrived.

With thousands of sightings, already recorded researchers are certain that a future drought will bring another spate of sightings. Academics and bureaucrats in their urban environment will continue to insist that there is no evidence to support witness reports of "big cats". Farmers will look at their slaughtered livestock and wonder just how much proof is necessary.

It is apparent that a large, nocturnal carnivore is roaming the Australian countryside. This creature is killing and eating native wildlife as well as domestic stock. It is capable of killing even adult cattle and can devour a whole full-grown sheep or large kangaroo at a single sitting. The method of eating its prey is indicative of only one Australian predator that was **ever** known to exist **Thylacoleo Carnifex.**

Chapter 9

Sightings are so common in the Maryborough Vic district that locals have added images to various road signs to indicate areas where the animals are regularly seen. Despite the fact that people regularly say they have seen a panther or a puma, it is likely they have seen a thylacoleo but not knowing that such an animal exists people apply a name that fits what they witnessed.

Sightings are extremely common in the Daisy Hill area as the region is between the Maryborough State Park and the Paddy's Ranges National Park. It is assumed the animals are crossing farmland between these two forests on a regular basis.

Chapter 10

The find in Witchcliffe, WA has revealed the marsupial lion could climb extraordinarily well, and may have raised its young in caves. Flinders University palaeontologists have been attempting to discern more of the behaviour of this giant predator which is believed by scientists to have become extinct thousands of year ago. Much about **Thylacoleo Carnifex** remains a mystery.

It was robust. It had enormously powerful meat-scissor teeth. It also had a fearsome retractable thumb claw thought to be used to tear out the throat or disembowel its prey.

Scientists are still unsure whether marsupial lions could climb trees and leap onto unsuspecting prey. The Aboriginals have no doubt of this ability nor do many witnesses but as the scientists are restricted to working with long deceased animals it is difficult for them to reach a conclusion. Whether they were solitary or social is still not fully determined; and whether adults left young behind in dens when they went off to feed like other carnivores such as Tasmanian devils and hyenas is part of the story yet to be established, according to **Associate Professor Gavin Prideaux** who said, "We cannot travel back in time to answer these questions and one can only deduce so much from fossil skeletons."

Fortunately, these animals left more than their bones lingering after their deaths.

It's long been inferred that marsupial lions, like all marsupials, gave birth to highly dependent young. These could not be left alone until they were sufficiently grown.

How Thylacoleo looked after its joeys once they left the pouch has long been a mystery which the Witchcliffe cave finds could well answer.

A thylacoleo skeleton displaying its distinctive large claw; Source: Gavin Prideaux / Flinders University

A model of the Thylacoleo Carnifex marsupial lion Picture: Paul Ovendon / Australian Museum

Thylacoleo Lives

Examining scratch marks in the cave researchers conclude, "The largest of the scratch marks could only have been made by adults of thylacoleo carnifex", researchers say. "Many of the smaller marks were made by juveniles: they have the same form as that of the adults, but do not match claw marks made by other known cave dwellers." It is believed that caves would have offered the cool and safe environment needed. Underground lairs also could be defended from other carnivores such as thylacines (Tasmanian tigers) and Tasmanian devils.

But the communal cave also supports another, significant, implication: "Given that marsupial lions were apparently adapted to apprehending and consuming large prey, it is feasible that they hunted cooperatively", the researchers say. If these researchers are correct and that thylacoleo was a cooperative hunter it would explain why an animal can be completely devoured in a single night. It does not explain why witnesses never report seeing more than one animal at a time. The few photographs and video clips we have are almost all of solitary animals. I have seen only one video clip that showed multiple animals, it showed a number of juvenile panther like animals playing together.

Cooperative hunting had previously been suggested by the discovery of bones bearing thylacoleo tooth-marks apparently from multiple animals at other sites; this could also explain why a prey animal could be completely stripped of flesh in a single night. The recent evidence supports the idea that the marsupial lions were stocky yet agile predators ideally suited to bringing down giant short-faced kangaroos and humans.

Evocative paintings of what are believed to be thylacoleos have been found in ancient Aboriginal rock art the most dramatic of which is in the northern Kimberly and shows a beast with heavy fore-shoulders leaping at man. It is feasible for them to have tackled mega fauna of the largest variety. Bones of the rhino-sized diprotodont have been found with thylacoleo bite-marks on them.

Despite the belief among palaeontologists that thylacoleo became extinct at the time of the demise of the mega-fauna there is ample evidence that thylacoleo lived at least until relatively recent times. Archaeologist Norman Tindale in his book "The Book of the Murray" wrote a summary of the animals that once roamed the Murray River catchment area and around the limestone caves of Swan Reach in Eastern Victoria.

"There were diprotodons as big as a rhinoceros and several species of giant kangaroo standing more than ten feet high." Mention was also made of thylacoleo, "a marsupial lion, with a large head and chisel like teeth, yet the body was no bigger than a merino ram. The bones of this creature were very hard and much sought after by the Aborigines who inhabited this area, because the tough bones were most acceptable for use in making their weapons. These people were the Negritis, later known as the Tartangans."

Dr Tindale wrote extensively on Aboriginal tribes and custom as well as various species of Australian fauna both current and historical. The fact that he ascertained that aboriginals were using the bones of thylacoleo to manufacture weapons implies that bones that were not fossilised were available in the Swan Reach area in modern times. It is logical to assume from this that at least in some regions thylacoleo evidently survived until modern times.

Chapter 11

Despite governments insisting that there are
no large predators in the Australian bush
farmers keep losing stock and people who
work or spend time in the bush continue to
see a variety of animals. Those compiling a
data base in NSW have over 270 eyewitness
reports and Victorian groups have many
more. This is not an indication of a greater
number of animals just that Victoria has
many areas that are not as rugged as the
main habitat in NSW so the animals are not
able to as easily hide.

In addition to groups and associations
collecting information many interested
individuals are compiling their own files. I
have discussed reports and exchanged
information with several of these people and
have collected a large number of very
reliable accounts. I will detail some of the

more interesting ones here, as although in early chapters I have listed a few sightings there are many others that go to help build the picture of our mysterious predator.

I only began collecting reports a little over thirty years ago even though some of my sightings predate this time. Some of the information I have been given also relates to sightings long before this time. An example of this is a report from the Ballarat Courier from July 1895 which reported a farmer seeing a "Tantanoola Tiger, whose roar resembles that of a lion crossed the road in front of him" at Nathalia in northern Victoria.

Other reports sent to me include from a March 1989 report in the Sunday Press "Two Ballarat forestry workers reported sighting a cat like animal at Lexton. In August 1989 the 'Lancefield Panther' was sighted at Riddells Creek. In June 1993 the

Seymour Gazette reported that Farm Manager Lyall Williams sighted a black big cat like animal at Strath Creek.

In December 2002 Binginwarri (South Gippsland), farmer Ron Jones reported a heifer killed by a panther. Mr. Jones said the heifer was partly eaten "like it had been cut with a carving knife", he also reported having seen the panther "about a dozen times". He described the animal as about three and a half feet (110 cm) from the ground to the top of the head when sitting on its haunches.

He told ABC Radio "When they take off they sort of go in big loping bounds. They cover about twenty feet (six metres) every bound; they're about eight feet (2.6 metres) from the tip of the nose to the end of their tail." Mr. Jones remained certain that he had witnessed a big cat that looked exactly like a black panther.

A Central Highlands Water Board employee informed me of several sightings he had experienced. His position entailed inspecting water board assets and equipment in various locations at reservoirs and along the pipelines, on several occasions he saw "panthers" found killed and eaten kangaroos and tracks of a large predator. His most interesting sighting however came one night after he and his wife had visited friends for a night of playing cards.

They were driving home and as they crested a hill saw the animal beside the road. It took off bounding along the side of the road but it only took a couple of seconds to arrive at the road beside the running animal. Their utility drew next to the animal whose head was about level with the window sill and he said to his wife, "Reach out and grab it." To which she responded, "You grab it." By this time they had almost reached a bridge and the animal veered down an embankment and into the scrub along the banks of the creek.

A sighting near Maryborough was also interesting in that it is another confirmation of the thylacoleo climbing trees. A young lad had been walking his dog in the forest and as it was coming on for dusk he began to head home. On a paddock near the edge of the forest he saw a small mob of kangaroos grazing, they stood and watched him nervously and when the dog moved toward them they took flight.

Within seconds of them taking off across the paddock a large black panther jumped from a nearby tree and pursued them. The lad said his dog then lost all interest and was eager to continue for home.

Chapter 12

In addition to reports of panther like animals we often receive reports of striped animals, some of which are cat-like similar to our panther-like animal others are thylacine or Tasmanian tiger. Due to the number of Tasmanian tiger sightings I will devote this chapter primarily to that animal, although it seems that there is some overlap in identification as some thylacoleos may be striped. A very good report was given to me of an animal that was seen in 1967 and was positively identified as a Tasmanian tiger.

The witness and his wife were returning home at about 2:15 AM through Mt Helen toward Bunninyong which is not far from Ballarat. The area was sparsely populated in those days and an animal leapt from the embankment on the right and ran across the road toward a dam. Both the man and his wife witnessed the animal and agreed that it was without doubt a thylacine; although it was dark the animal was well illuminated by the car's headlights.

On telling neighbours of the sighting they were greeted with laughter and disbelief. The man was even more surprised about a month later when returning home alone at about 1:00 AM he saw the same (?) animal at the same place sitting on the embankment. This time he stopped and moved the car into a position where the lights were directly on the animal and watched it for over two minutes.

This was a sufficient time to carefully examine the animal and be completely certain that the animal was a thylacine. The neighbours again laughed until one of them was going to work at 4:00 AM the next week and also saw the animal at the same place. This person managed to watch the thylacine for "about fifteen minutes", no further reports have come from this area since.

The same witness tells of meeting an old resident of Ozenkadnook, the region of Rilla Martin's famous photograph, around 1964 which is about the same time as Rilla's photo was released. He asked this resident, "Have you ever seen the tiger?" The resident replied, "Yes three times young feller; once after the Queen died, (Queen Victoria died in 1901) once in 1914 and once in 1943 or 44." It was also commented that all of these were drought years; as recorded earlier sightings increase in drought years when the animals are forced to look for water.

In April 1995 Sunday Herald Sun ran an article following a spate of tiger, puma, and panther sightings. A livestock hauler and his mate saw a Tasmanian tiger near Penshurst. The men said they saw it clearly and described the circumstances, "We were driving down Stonefield Lane (which is about five kilometres long) to unload steers from the Hamilton saleyards. The creature jumped across the road from our right... We pulled up; the animal went among the sheep and cattle. It didn't spook the cattle, the calves didn't move. It stood side on, allowing us a clear view.

The creature was as tall as a greyhound but twice as thick. Its big snout tapered, its rear legs were set forward of the tail. Where it joined the body the tail was so thick a man's hand wouldn't go round it. The legs leaned inwards twenty degrees off the vertical. Stripes on its body gradually became obvious, about two inches wide and of a yellowy-orange colour on a dark base."

There were other reports that occurred about the same time; a lady reported seeing one about fifty kilometres away that same week and a Hamilton stock agent saw an animal several days later at Dunkeld. The agent did not notice stripes but the animal appeared to be a uniform dark colour.

Another Dunkeld resident said he saw a pitch-black puma after it killed one of his chickens. "I took up my 12 gauge shotgun but it vanished like a streak." A farmer south of Dunkeld was "going around the sheep in my 4WD I looked up and there it was strolling along about sixty metres ahead; a big black cat-like animal. I gave chase across the paddocks for a kilometre. I was doing 80 kmh just keeping it in sight. When I topped a rise it had vanished."

This same farmer's brother-in-law lives at Mirrinattwa at the foot of the Grampians and has encountered "three different kinds" of big cat over the years. "One was striped like a tiger; one similar to a lion in size and shape, fawny-grey like an unsheared sheep; the third was black as a puma".

A particularly reliable report of a Tasmanian tiger sighting was sent to another researcher in a letter from a lady in Tasmania. In 1978 in the far North West of Tasmania she witnessed a thylacine with only the width of the highway between her and the animal. The reliability of this report is enhanced by the fact that the animal was seen by at least seven other people over period of several days. A couple of the witnesses were elderly bush-men who had seen tigers when they were more plentiful in the 1920's and confirmed the identification.

Chapter 13

Many reports are received concerning puma sightings, some of which claim to have seen black pumas. Black or melanistic pumas are not entirely unknown but are rare; melanism is the opposite of albinism and even if it was occurring it would be unlikely to produce a large population of animals of a single colour.

There is evidence that pumas are established in the Grampians mountain range a fact confirmed by a university study and countless eyewitnesses. It is believed that most of these pumas were released by US servicemen during WWII, but since then the population has expanded. Reports of sightings have come from as East as the Barwon River near Geelong; as far West as the SA border and as far North as Melville Caves, just South of Wedderburn. The extent of the range to the South is not known but the area is rugged and heavily forested in parts so a large population could remain undetected.

Even in the USA which is the puma's home range the animals prove elusive. Researchers in Montana reported that at one time no wild pumas were seen for a period of two years, despite researchers knowing that there was a good population of them in that state.

Late in 1994 following a spate of sightings of big cats, both pumas and panthers, the Ballarat Courier ran a three page article of witness reports and researchers comments. Being one of those who was featured by the paper I subsequently received a lot of extra mail and information. One letter from the town of Meredith, between Ballarat and Geelong, stated that, "My father came face to face with a puma ... [snipped] then I saw a puma when I was rabbiting. Both my father and I had a clear view of the animal. That is

how we were able to identify the animal as a
puma."

Chapter 14

In August 2002 the Sunday Herald Sun ran an article revealing leaked documents that revealed fifty-nine sightings of Victoria's black panthers. The paper stated the files had sparked claims of an X-files type cover up over livestock predation in Gippsland. The government did eventually hold an inquiry but concluded that there was no evidence of large predators in the state. Government is still refusing to accept eyewitness accounts or slaughtered livestock as evidence.

Included in the file was a report from 1999 when a "dogger", a hunter employed to hunt wild dogs for the Department of Natural Resources, reported a "huge black puma-size cat" seen at Seaton near Heyfield. The dogger wrote "I got a shot at it with a rifle from about three hundred yards. I hit the animal but it did not stop it. It disappeared into a thick patch of black-berries. Days and days of searching the area failed to find any trace of the animal." Many of the reported sightings took place over periods of five minutes or more with the longest over twenty minutes, my own sighting lasted even longer.

Sightings have been reported by many different people from all walks, apart from the dogger many rural workers, people familiar with animals, have seen them. Most sightings are in the bush or on farmland. The animals have also been seen crossing roads as well as by a school bus driver and his passengers and a group of seven prisoners with a prison guard from Wron Wron jail. Despite these multiple witness reports the government still refuses to admit the animals exist.

In 2010 the National Party agreed to conduct an investigation should the coalition win office. They won and the Department of Sustainability and the Environment (DSE) released their findings in August 2012. The investigation was triggered because a Melbourne based investigator obtained documents under the Freedom of Information Act that revealed dozens of sightings across the state.

The then Labour Environment Minister of course derided the effort to find out what was there and suggested that it was a waste of effort but if they find a Dodo or a Unicorn he will give them the number of the zoo. With that he labelled all witnesses as liars or mistaken and confused, refusing to take seriously any part of the investigation. Despite the derision of the Labour Party the enquiry proceeded; the results will be examined in a later chapter.

Chapter 15

Most of the information in this book has referred to sightings in Victoria but as mentioned previously sightings do occur in all states. Fossilised remains have been found in all states indicating that thylacoleo was as widespread as its primary prey, the kangaroo. In a previous chapter I also alluded to researchers in NSW who had collected details of almost three hundred eyewitness accounts.

Many of these are identical to Victorian sightings and the most commonly reported animal is a black panther like animal. Just like the Victorian government the NSW government also refuses to take sightings or predation seriously.

Reports or sightings from Queensland are particularly fascinating because of the variety of animals witnesses claim to have observed. The Black Panther does not appear to be as common in the warmer climes and in the far North in tropical rainforests a tan or sandy coloured tree climbing animal is reported.

James Cook University researcher Scott Burnett was in the Atherton Tablelands to research the endangered Spotted-tail quoll. He collected local fauna reports from long time residents, particularly those involved in timber cutting or tin mining. Witnesses described a sandy coloured animal the size of a dingo with a rounded head and small ears.

The locals were aware of the quoll but had also seen another creature in rocky areas of the rainforest. It was described as a solitary animal not a pack animal that hunted rather than scavenged and could climb trees. The animal's description was remarkably similar to a mysterious animal described by naturalist Carl Lumholtz who explored North Queensland in the 1880's. Lumholtz used the knowledge of local Aborigines to identify four species then unknown to science; including the tree kangaroo. His search for the animal that the Aborigines described as sandy coloured, the size of a dingo, savage and able to climb trees; was unsuccessful, Lumholtz believed the animal may have been a marsupial tiger.

University researcher Scott Burnett told the press, "We know marsupial lions once roamed Australia, it is not inconceivable that an elusive creature could have survived largely undetected." Since those first reports Scott has found accounts of a similar animal from Millaa Millaa and Mt. Carbine as well as mysterious tracks on Mount Bartle Frere.

The density of forests in many parts of Australia is such that one could be invisible at a little more than a metre off a road or track. Tropical rainforests are dense with a large variety of shrubs and vines, forests in cooler climates have thick patches of ferns of many varieties. Melaleuca, protea, coffee bush, and wattles of various types provide underbrush in open forests. There is a lot of cover available for an animal that wishes to remain unseen. There is little doubt that the researcher's belief that an animal could remain undiscovered is an accurate assessment.

Chapter 16

In the light of numerous eyewitness reports and the evidence of killed and devoured livestock thousands of farmers and other rural residents know that these animals exist because they have seen them or the result of their attacks. The reasons governments still refuse to acknowledge their existence is best defined by the Victorian government report of August 2012.

Although my submission was not included in the assessment I was given a copy of the report. The report is subject to copyright so I cannot simply reproduce it for readers but can summarise and comment. The report is titled, "Assessment of evidence for the Presence in Victoria of a Wild Population of 'big cats'". The report was compiled by Peter W Menkhorst and Leigh Morison of the Arthur Rylah Institute for Environmental Research. The report is available as a PDF on the internet at www.dse.vic.gov.au for those who would like their own copy.

The summary begins by declaring that there are no records of big cats in any databases managed by the Victorian Government or its agencies; despite many decades of research and monitoring. The summary does acknowledge that there are "many thousands" of reports of sightings and evidence of predation in the files of community groups and individuals.

Because the evidence consists of primarily eyewitness accounts and killed and eaten livestock and wildlife this is inconclusive without further corroborating evidence. The truthfulness or accuracy of witness accounts cannot be accepted without material evidence. The report's explanation for many reported sightings is that they are large feral cats; it does acknowledge that some evidence and behaviours are outside the ability of known predators in Victoria. It also suggests however that our understanding of known predator behaviour might be inadequate. This in the view of the report is the most logical explanation.

This of course implies that feral cats and foxes are responsible for killing and devouring full grown sheep as well as cattle and horses. I am sure that there are farmers who have seen the injuries inflicted on their livestock imagining giant feral cats causing the damage many of us have witnessed.

The report acknowledges that domestic cats have been recorded to weights of sixteen kilograms although studies show that most cats are between two and six kilograms. It is difficult to imagine even a sixteen kilogram feral cat bringing down full grown one hundred kilogram sheep or a five hundred to thousand kilogram horse or cow; surely even the most desk bound researcher could ascertain this without even going to look at the animals. A similar expectation would apply to foxes, dogs and predatory birds.

The government inquiry also concludes that should a big cat be shot or captured "more than one specimen would be required because a single individual is not evidence of a self-sustaining population". The study is preparing the position for denial of the existence of these animals even if a specimen is obtained. I would argue of course that if the specimen recovered was uniquely Australian such as thylacoleo it would be impossible to deny a living population. A single animal could not have existed for thousands of years; a breeding population must linger.

Chapter 17

The government assessment acknowledges that a wild population of big cats would have serious economic consequences for farming, the ecology, conservation and possibly public safety. It is for these reasons many believe the government is playing down the reports and possible existence of such an apex predator.

Despite the evidence of predation that is outside the capabilities of known predators and scavengers such as foxes, dogs, domestic cats, pigs, birds and goannas the report suggests that these animals may be responsible as our knowledge of their feeding habits may be inadequate. Again I doubt that the farming community is unfamiliar with the feeding habits of foxes, dogs, domestic cats, pigs, birds and goannas and is likely to mistake the work of a large carnivore for the predation of any of these creatures. It is my view that the investigators are deliberately understating the intelligence of the community at large as a reason to reject the possibility of large cat-like predators in the Australian bush.

The report also notes that no species of cat is native to Australia and only *Felis catus,* the domestic cat, is known to have established a self sustaining population in Australia. The key word here is 'known' this does not exclude other members of the cat family as having created populations; albeit in smaller numbers than the domestic cat.

Despite knowing that there are large numbers of wild domestic cats and foxes in the bush these are not often seen. Hunters using spotlights and fox whistles often manage to locate and shoot members of both species.

During lambing season farmers and hunters have been known to easily bag thirty or forty foxes in a single evening of shooting. I have on occasion shot wild cats on properties we have owned, or had my Staghound cross hunting dog catch them and bite them in half. The point of this is to demonstrate that despite large numbers of both foxes and cats these things are not often seen; more elusive predators are far less likely to be found.

The government assessment also points out that rumours of 'big cats' come from many other countries including Britain, Ireland, Finland Denmark and even New Zealand and so claim that it is a form of pareidolia or urban myth and is more a human social problem than a biological fact. A number of groups and individuals in Victoria have compiled large collections of reports, and photographs. This as well as media interest is being blamed for the widespread belief particularly in rural communities in the existence of big cats and panthers in the Australian bush. This assumption of course ignores the fact that most long time residents in rural communities have either seen these animals, seen the result of attacks on livestock or know of friends or family who have seen them.

It is very difficult for people who have seen these animals to accept that they were just imagining them or were seeing a feral cat. The witness who was driving beside a panther like animal whose head was close to the window of his car cannot be convinced that it was just feral cat. The animal that I saw through the telescopic sight of my rifle was not even a cat, let alone a feral. It was also about 90 cm tall at the shoulder, too large to be mistaken for another animal; but sufficiently cat-like to be mistaken for a cat at any distance more than a couple of metres. The report classifies these reports as 'convictions' by people that they have seen a large cat-like animal but without evidence disregards sightings as mistakes or some form of confusion.

Personal testimony is disregarded as unreliable. Despite the fact that many reports come from people with vast experience and very responsible positions. Included in the list of witnesses are police officers, forestry officials, veterinary surgeon and employees, a zookeeper who actually had owned panther and thought his animal had escaped as well as farmers and train drivers.

Many years ago I even received a report from a titled gentleman who made me pledge never to reveal his name as a condition revealing what he saw. The attitude of government and many in society is such that it discourages the reporting of sightings and people become wary of being ridiculed if their information is made public.

This particular gentleman described what could only be a large but juvenile puma that he saw while attending a function near Beaufort in Central Victoria.

Chapter 18

The report divides the type of evidence needed to convince authorities into three categories. Primary evidence would be a specimen, skeletal material, teeth, fur or DNA. Secondary evidence is broken into two parts a) sighting supported by photographs, video or audio recording, and b) unsupported sighting. Most sightings fall into the category of secondary b) and so carry little weight with government officials.

The third type of evidence is Tertiary evidence and is sign that an animal has been present. This might consist of tracks, scats, predated remains or scratching. Samples collected in some cases from this type of evidence have been analysed for DNA but most have been inconclusive. One scat sample from north of the Otway Ranges was analysed to be felid but not positively identified. The possibility that the DNA was that of a panther could not be ruled out.

Sightings and reports that involve only secondary or tertiary evidence of animals that are not in the official databases cannot be accepted as evidence of existence. Only an animal whose existence is supported by primary evidence such as a museum specimen can be considered as certain to exist.

It is apparent that no matter how many witnesses see or report these animals their existence will not be accepted by authorities until a specimen is brought in dead or alive to the museum. It is unfortunate that most photographic evidence is of relatively poor quality but witnesses are afraid to approach these animals because of their large size.

The report concludes that the 'big cats' in Victoria only fit the size description of leopard, puma or jaguar, There is no scientific definition for 'panther' but the name is generally applied to melanistic members of the leopard or jaguar species. Black leopards and jaguars generally are not completely black but usually the spots are faintly visible in a deeper intensity than the main colour.

The animal in the Australian bush commonly referred to as a 'panther' or sometimes 'bush panther' is totally black. Sometimes described as shiny black to quote one witness, "It was black and shiny like the wing of a crow." This colouration differs from that seen in most members of the leopard or jaguar families. Feral cats also come in a variety of colours including tabby, ginger and black often with white markings; there is no reason to expect that all large specimens would be black.

Based on colour alone it becomes probable that we are dealing with a species that is unrelated to any known felid genus. The government report avoids any thought that large cat-like animals could be anything but a cat. Marsupials can easily be mistaken for other species; possums for example often look like domestic cats when moving on the ground.

There was a story popularised on social media of a group of Asian students who advertised for the owner of a lost cat they had found. The photograph they included had Australians laughing; the 'lost cat' was quite obviously a possum.

If the animal commonly seen and referred to as a 'panther' is actually a thylacoleonid it is to be expected that witnesses would classify it as a big cat, simply because the prevailing opinion is that thylacoleo is extinct. An animal that is as large as a melanistic leopard and of an almost identical shape is automatically categorised as that until further evidence is obtained to contradict the initial observation.

In my observation near Tarnagulla I was convinced the animal was a member of the genus panthera, which includes leopards and tigers, right up until I was looking at the face through the telescopic sight on my rifle. It was only at that point did I gain enough evidence to know that I was not stalking a cat.

The government sponsored assessment also speculates that people may be mistaking black wallabies, very common in Victoria for big black cats. If a witness only saw a part of the animal moving through the bush that theory may be possible, but anyone seeing the forepaws would never mistake a wallaby for a cat. Many of our witnesses give very clear descriptions, not only of the forepaws but of the entire body shape. Broad chested and with thick muscular forelegs could never describe a wallaby, but is often used to describe large cat-like animals.

Chapter 19

The official assessment of big cats also examined the Deakin University study of the existence of pumas in the Grampians. The government began by suggesting that by calling the university project the "Deakin Puma Study" the participants were influenced to read puma into evidence that had no connection to pumas.

That claim of bias of course ignores the main reason the study was commenced. It only began because of numerous reports of pumas being seen in the Grampians area. The Deakin report was further harmed by the claim that a scat was from a puma when in fact Monash University zoologists identified it as a regurgitated pellet from a wedge-tailed eagle.

The only evidence that the report acknowledges cannot be disputed is that of clear footprints photographed in Longford Pine Plantation. The prints are undeniably from a cat and far too large to be attributed to a feral domestic cat. I have personally seen cat scratchings on trees near Creswick that are 140 cm (4 ft) from the ground, that is also far too high to have been made by a feral domestic cat.

Cat scratching 140 cm from the ground near Creswick

Despite these few unexplained examples the investigation can go no further. The report recommends that there is insufficient evidence to warrant spending public funds on further investigation. That of course is the crux of the matter, not to warrant spending money on this research. The government is still happy to have groups and individuals spend their own time and money trying to obtain primary evidence.

Chapter 20

The government investigation observes that although some departments are now using infra-red cameras to photograph wildlife no big cat or other unknown species has yet been photographed. It might be in the government's interest to claim that this lack of evidence is evidence of lack; but it might just as likely be that the cameras have been poorly located. Some conspiracy theorists argue that any images captured would be kept secret.

Reliance of ground based cameras may not be adequate if we are dealing with an arboreal thylacoleonid. The animals are regularly sighted on the ground but also seem able to move through trees; as witnesses report from the Grampians region in Victoria as well as in Queensland. An animal that hunts by ambush from a tree may not spend as much time on the ground as might be assumed and so not be photographed by a ground based camera.

Many of the sightings of animals on the ground occur in areas away from forests, so ground based cameras in forest areas might be poorly placed to capture an image of a thylacoleo. In forests the animal can move through trees but if no trees are present the animal is forced to move along the ground, as do koalas and other arboreal marsupials.

The government report is an excuse for the government not to fund research into the existence of large predators. The best groups and individuals can hope for is to obtain some form of sponsorship to continue the research. If organisations such as National Geographic or a film company could be enticed into joining the search the required equipment might be obtained.

Instead of ground based trail cameras good infra-red imaging cameras like those used in police helicopters are more likely to produce results. I am certain that areas where there are many sightings could be flown over with either a helicopter or a drone. It might only take a very short time for an animal to be located.

Once located the animal could be followed to its daytime retreat where proper surveillance could be established. If the animal could be observed undisturbed we might fairly quickly ascertain many of its habits and range. The other option might be to sedate and tag the animal to enable observation.

A farmer who lived near Carisbrook in Central Victoria reported seeing a 'panther' on a regular basis. He knew that it lived on his property as he would regularly see it early in the mornings when it would go into a patch of trees growing beside a creek on his property. The animal did not come out and there was little ground cover for it to hide as his livestock had kept the area trimmed.

On several occasions he took his gun and went down to find it but was never able. He claimed that he did hear it several times and even though the sound was close he could never locate the animal. It is my belief that the animal was managing to hide in foliage overhead and keep out of sight. It would only have become obvious if it had dislodged a branch or knocked down enough leaves or bark to attract attention.

It is very obvious that these animals see people far more often than people see them. We can only hope that some corporate sponsor or wealthy good citizen will aid with the funding required to prove the existence of these elusive predators. I have had people tell me that they have had the feeling of being watched while in the local forest, whether this is by an animal or person nobody knows.

There are many koalas in the Maryborough district but in the last twenty-five years I have only seen them on half a dozen occasions. Only one koala has been killed on local roads in that time; so a lack of road killed animals in the case of a more agile animal is cannot be an excuse to deny the existence of the animal. The only time we find koalas easily is early in the morning when they can sometimes be found feeding on the leaves of small young trees. Later in the day they will be sleeping high in large trees and can take a lot of searching to locate.

An arboreal nocturnal predator could be even more difficult to locate than a koala. Despite many years of trying to discern the habits of these mysterious animals we have only just scratched the surface. By sharing information with other researchers we have built up a reasonable idea of the more obvious behaviours but have only touched the surface of what is needed to obtain positive proof.

Chapter 21

Despite government denial 'panther' sightings continue to be reported. In Maryborough we receive reports continually many from places close to town.

One young man reported coming face to face with a panther that was drinking from a dam behind the power sub-station right on the edge of town.

A resident close to the area of the Bristol Hill Tower, a local landmark, arose early one morning and received the surprise of his life when he looked out his kitchen window. There in the forest just beyond his back fence was a panther-like animal strolling along behind the houses.

On the opposite side of town on Majorca Road some houses back onto the forest, a resident told me of an experience they had one morning. At the back of their block is a shed where stock feed and equipment is stored, his daughter went down to collect some requirements from the shed but returned moments later calling out, "Dad, there's a panther in the shed."

By the time he grabbed a weapon and ran down there the animal had escaped into the scrub beyond the fence. The daughter had been so frightened that she had not taken the time to examine the animal and could only really say that it was very big and black.

Following an election the electoral officers worked quite late counting votes and securing the ballots to ensure there could be no interference and did not finish until about midnight. On the way home to Carisbrook one of the officers was surprised by a panther running across the road.

Fortunately she rang me the next morning with accurate details and I was able to go out early and locate where the animal had come out of the forest and crossed the road. The tracks were quite clear and I was able to follow for quite some distance. The animal had come from the forest and travelled in a large circle before returning to the forest. Approximately mid-way along this route it had killed and eaten a wallaby and only a small amount of skin and bones were left.

I endeavoured to follow into the forest to find where the animal might be spending its days but unfortunately I lost the tracks on some rocky ground and leaf litter. I circled around trying to recover the tracks to no avail and assume the animal may have taken to the trees, if it was the species I suspected; and which the tracks indicated.

Also close to town was a sighting of my own. Although I was retired when a local bakehouse was expanding I offered my services. Although they were a little reluctant about hiring someone who was already in his late sixties they needed someone to start so I got the job. I worked there for three years but eventually had to retire again as one seems to begin to lose a little stamina once you pass seventy.

I began on night shift but soon switched to afternoon shift which meant I would knock off about 11:00 PM but on occasion worked overtime finishing as late as 3:00 AM. On one of these late finishes I left work and headed toward home, at the end of the road from the factory there is a T intersection and the land opposite is part of a flora reserve.

As I approached the intersection my headlights shone deep into the reserve and there walking through the reserve was a panther-like animal. Being familiar with the species and its dimensions I recognised it instantly. It was too far from the road to try and pursue, but it looked directly at my car and then went nonchalantly on its way. I went and bought a dash-cam but the inconsiderate beast did not return.

If I was to delay publication of this book I would no doubt be able to present many more interesting anecdotes but they will not sway opinion one little bit. We can only hope that in the not too distant future someone will obtain a good photograph or will shoot one.

Meanwhile to all those farmers, forestry workers, stock agents and prospectors please keep your guns and cameras ready, one way or another we will obtain the proof. I sometimes regret not shooting the one at Tarnagulla when I had the chance, the argument would be over; then I think no I am glad I didn't shoot it. I would much rather have good quality photographs or video than to kill such a magnificent animal.

Thylacoleo Lives

Acknowledgements

Usually at this point I would list the names of those who have contributed information and witness reports. The list is so extensive that I would have pages that looked like a telephone directory. I would therefore simply like to express my thanks to all those who have seen these animals and had the courage to speak up, despite ridicule and denial from many in the community and in government.

To all those who have kept records of sightings and shared information; and to those who have maintained web-pages, forums, social media sites and data bases they have shared a special thank you.

Thylacoleo Lives

About the author

Dennis Wright was born in Melbourne where his engineer father was employed during WWII. His Mother's family had come from Great Western in Victoria's west and his Father's family was from Kyneton in central Victoria.

Soon after the war, his father purchased a general store west of Melbourne but after a couple of years moved to a country property at Reedy Creek in the upper Goulburn Valley. The author has since resided in rural Victoria for most of his life, apart from a period when he was studying and then employed in Melbourne. He has travelled extensively throughout Australia; his employment has taken him to every capital city and to countless rural centres.

Now retired he lives with his wife in Maryborough in Central Victoria. His extended family includes their children, grandchildren and great-grandchildren. Apart from researching unusual animals and physics he spends time writing books, fishing and prospecting for gold. Once also a keen shooter and sailor he does little of either today.

Thylacoleo Lives

Thylacoleo Lives

Thylacoleo Lives

Thylacoleo Lives

www.ingramcontent.com/pod-product-compliance
Lightning Source LLC
Chambersburg PA
CBHW071404280526
45787CB00001B/425